D1190139

With a good reporter's precision and a gifted poet's empathy, Jeanne Bryner's latest book, focuses on "the epic of everyday life." Here, she recreates the story of her husband, her children, the roof and doors of her house, her unpredictable garden, and her farmer neighbor's crops and cattle. Beneath this deceptively simple tale lies an undertow of sorrow, as well as the frisson of joy and laughter necessary to sustain a long marriage, deep looking, and an engaged life. Like a contemporary Ovid, Bryner uses her considerable powers of metaphor to transform everything in these poems into something else. Here, gulls become boys, small animals become vegetables and people are trees. Even a tree's shadow "walks in stiff trousers." Haunted and haunting, *Both Shoes Off* is a true gift from a wise and accomplished poet, straight from the "good bones church" of her remarkable life.

—Maggie Anderson, Author of *Windfall: New and Selected Poems* and Founding Director of the Wick Poetry Center at Kent State University

OTHER BOOKS BY JEANNE BRYNER

Early Farming Woman, Finishing Line Press (2014)

Smoke: Poems, Bottom Dog Press (2012)

No Matter How Many Windows, Wind Publications (2010)

Tenderly Lift Me: Nurses Honored, Celebrated, and Remembered, Kent State University Press (2004)

Eclipse: Stories, Bottom Dog Press (2003)

Blind Horse: Poems, Bottom Dog Press (1999)

Breathless, Kent State University Press (1995)

BOTTOM DOG PRESS

BOTH SHOES OFF

JEANNE BRYNER

Jeanne Bryner (handwritten signature)

2-16-20 For Karen, On a sunny February day @ TMU, Jeanne (handwritten inscription)

HARMONY WRITING SERIES
BOTTOM DOG PRESS
HURON, OHIO

© 2016 Jeanne Bryner
and Bottom Dog Press
ISBN 978-1-933964-84-3
Bottom Dog Press
PO Box 425, Huron, Ohio 44839
http://smithdocs.net

First Edition

General Editor: Susanna Sharp-Schwacke
Associate Editor: Larry Smith
Layout and Cover Design: Susanna Sharp-Schwacke
Cover Image: *Carol's Farm*, Judy Waid

ACKNOWLEDGMENTS

Many thanks to the editors of the publications in which the following poems previously appeared, sometimes in slightly different forms: "Killdeer" and "Blue Mason Jar" in *Appalachian Journal*; "Gray Wool Carpet," and "Swimming Hole" in *Bliss: A Poetry Anthology*, eds. Jim and Jean Anton, Muse Press, 2013; "Paper" limited edition broadside, Camino Press, 2013; "Milkweed" and "Those Boys Who Were Fourteen" in *Changing Harm to Harmony,* ed. Joseph Zaccardi, 2015; "Christmas Lights on My Neighbor's Silo," "Homeroom Poet Mom: For the Second Graders, Catholic Elementary, 1989," "Locust Shell" in *A Poetry Congeries*; "August 1976: Bertha Welcomes Me to the Neighborhood" and "Watching My Neighbor in His Fields" in *Every River on Earth: Writing From Appalachian Ohio,* ed. Neil Carpathios, OU Press, 2015; "Photo Journalist," "The Garden in Winter," and "Violets" in *Hektoen International: A Journal of Medical Humanities*; "Gourd" in *Jawbone*; "Erasers" in *Ohio Poetry Association* anthology; "Why It Happens" in *Poetry East*; "At the Heart Doctor's Office, I Take the Last Seat" in *Still: The Journal*; "I Have Only A Broom Handle" in *Words*; and "Dusk" in *World Literature Today*.

Continued on page 109.

CONTENTS

For Merle McCord St. Clair and Carl St. Clair

I think of how it goes on,
this dark particular bent of our hungers:
the way wire eats into a tree
year after year on the pasture's perimeter,
keeping milk cows penned
until they grow too old to freshen.
                                        —Maxine Kumin
                                        "How It Goes On"

The Lord said to Moses: 'Remove the
sandals from your feet, for the place
where you stand is holy ground.'
                                        —Acts 7:33

GULLS IN THE CORNFIELD

All of their wings are bruised
and with their coats blown open,
my husband says they are young boys

running home from school,
hurrying to throw down books,
grab a fist full of cookies, gulp milk from a jug.

His eyes are worse than mine.

Far from the ocean,
caught now in hay bracken,
they seem to search for a map,
any compass to point them back.

There appears no captain, just rowdy
sailors milling about the great basin
of my neighbor's cornfield. They pitch and swagger,

screech and scream into each other's face. And while
no punches land, it makes me think they drank
last night. Still, I have seen them in dress whites,

loved them when they are not so manic,
watched them rise and fan out,
a lace tablecloth blowing easy on a line.

Without partners, they have learned to waltz.

Against a blackboard of winter trees, bodies
take the shapes of letters, a lonely, crazy alphabet
a language only the homeless know.

Mom, please send socks.
Dad, did you find me a transmission?
What? You want to date other guys?

The mail's so slow, they just keep writing.

A great mystery, their suspension, mid-air,
how we both landed next to barns and calves
far from any warm sea breeze, salty taste of waves
no wonder they cry.

I.

Vergil from down the road
steps out of his pickup truck,

throws open the big red gate.
The hay has been mowed and baled,

the meadow ready for new foragers.
In a stately line, like the entry of royalty,

hogs and sheep go into the pasture.
                    —Irene McKinney
                              "Pastoral"

The Oxen

We went to our wagon,
two orphans reaching for the nuns,

starved for sweetness, born again
in those covers where we slept closer

than spoons in a drawer,
our backs turned away from knives.

Still, we bought a saw, stacks
of wood, stuff to fix walls.

And how many board feet
of maple, pine, oak did I catch

on the backside of its teeth?
Shavings dancing like fireflies

in our hair, incense of heart wood
lulling us careless, making us unafraid.

But able blades (more than once)
caught us both. Forty years? Hulls

of empty bandage boxes, blood
puddles leading up the stairs.

The blue plates we threw
at each other? The ones stamped

I don't love you anymore?
We swept them up, buried them

on the trail. Soft gauze bound
our eyes, hands-to-shoulders

we staggered through coiled dark.
Now, many good doctors, pills.

Any pain you cannot bear,
I will carry until we become the light.

August 1976:
Bertha Welcomes Me to the Neighborhood

A sweet voice calls
from the screen door's other side.

Her apron's alive, blooms buttercups.
Just as short as my grandmother, she
wears her plain gray hair, sensible shoes,
a white slip under her dress.

Her arms cradle twin zucchini, ripe
tomatoes and squash, like a sleeping baby.
Near a tangled path of boxes, I stumble
over nouns, used newspapers,
chew and chew stale gum.

I'm surprised when she asks
about my washer, our well.
Automatics take a lot of water—
be careful—
(she points to the floor).
This here's a hand-dug well.

Her tone lifts my chin.
I try to swallow the gum,
Yes ma'am. I reply, sliding
down inside my skin
the only desk I've got.

Bertha, please forgive the lateness
of this note, I believe
extraordinary
is the word I tried to find
the day you walked into a mess
saying, *Honey, just sit down,*
for work will not go away.
Thanks for a full afternoon
of your stories; they still

taste like warm berry pie
with sugar sprinkled crust,
kindness carried forward
on your way to the moon.

FARMER PHYSICIAN:
WHEN WE CUT OUR PLUM TREES DOWN

We listened when Theo spoke,
neighbor, farmer, friend, doctor without pills.

We took no joy in clearing the orchard,
cutting a dozen plum trees down.

Jam I'd imagined for biscuits,
honey smells planned for my stove.

Against the limbs' tender membrane
my husband's axe buries itself, reappears.

This farm running beside us provides
a daily magic show, calves born, cows fed,

but it's not the rest home's breath.
Harvest happens slow, also, stripping down.

Didn't Theo palpate each tree's spine,
slit puckered eyeballs with his knife

over the twig's dead eggs, shake his head,
declaring deafness in all their parts?

The plum trees? They're diseased.
No poultice can save them, now.

Merciful, how he did not feel vines
climbing beneath ribs and flannel shirt,

a sweet syrup rusting his pump,
four red feed bins grown soft.
      Theo's great good heart.

WATCHING MY NEIGHBOR IN HIS FIELDS

All the long morning, T-shirts, jeans blessed
over and over with sweat. My farmer
neighbor's an aging barber busy grooming
his fields' endless lines of rustling grass.

Below hay mist and yellow confetti puffs,
the tractor pulls, August heat drags him.
He holds on. It's a test of wills forcing stuff
to pack up and go; even grass knows it has

a place. At dusk, he leans against fence rails,
fingers laced, he chews grass like a used straw.
In evening air, bunnies and mice run over his body;
it lies yonder under the tractor's thrum.

And he's thrown his son into summer,
the deep blue end of its days, taught him
the hand ballet of its combs and scissors.
Looking forward, looking back, he cuts,

binds and loads. One eye on his mirror,
the other on the sky. Swim or sink, grass
is just another word for boys,
and they'll wrestle when caught for a trim.

The price of milk's down; all his sheds
are on their knees, still he brings us sweet
corn, plows our driveway for free. I shake
my head. Later, after calves get watered,

get fed, without grumbling, the farmer's son
swings himself to the tractor's high seat,
tines pass over the fields easy as a broom.
He hums and whistles as he sweeps

his father's floor. For almost nothing,
he cleans the church.

CHRISTMAS LIGHTS ON MY NEIGHBOR'S SILO

In December my neighbor's farm
sleeps late, reads mysteries
in bed, doesn't shave till Sunday.

For Christmas, his tractor and combine
have asked for new belts,
jazzy suspenders.

Hungry for company, they sit in the red
shed swapping lies, talking hip pain,
grease to ease it and weather.

They don't understand the farmer
stringing lights like a crown
'round the silo's head.

A risk to be walking clouds
and all those orange electric cords
snaking their way to the barn.

Every night no matter how fierce
or bitter the winds, after supper
the man rises, pulls on his boots

and thick coat, his cap with furry flaps.
He stops only to pet the calves, then
bends down, plugs in his lights.

Behind the snowflakes' gauzy curtains
a winter carousel,
his palette of colored lights

flying in the sky.
A miracle,
his young wife's pregnant
this is how happy they are.

WHY IT HAPPENS

I sit down on my blue glider to read Hemingway, as my neighbor, Susan, makes her fifth pass in the wheat field. Her combine's a chariot and she's a goddess, long yellow hair French braided down her back. She drives this giant machine the way guys named Stitch and Blade ram Harleys. If she knew I was here, sipping iced tea by my barrel of red geraniums, she'd wave.

She seems dressed like a waitress at Joe's lunch counter, as well she might be, coming from a steamy kitchen to take another order for fries and BLTs. In the windowed cab of the green machine, she holds her toddler daughter, Jenny, on her lap. Thrust and thrum of vibrating earth and gnawing grain shimmies through their warm thighs. What is it they share in this hazy space? Row after row of sunlight, riding this neck of growling dinosaur, do they sing above its grinding smell of grease? Does the child learn the many gears of silence?

Because I'm selfish, I moved to the country. I love the bouquet fragrance of new mown hay and watching lazy dirt trail farm tractors. I enjoy this without rising early for the fields. I can witness this without ordering spring seed and fretting over rainfall and hail storms. Clouds are white elephants to me. I work where air conditioners keep my mascara lines straight.

And when calving time comes, Susan invites us over to the barn. I take my daughter to see stalls convulse with blood and placentas and bawling. I explain biology cycles, birth, and why it happens like it does, why it all looks so messy. All the while, Susan holds Jenny astraddle her left hip, black rubber boots half stuck to straw, a dim light shines on their golden hair. Susan chews a piece of Juicy Fruit; Jenny smiles, sleepy on her mother's shoulder. They are not listening to me dwell on the delivery. The calf has started to get up: glistening, buckling, wet with his life.

ERASERS

Late August, traffic's heavy to the lake,
families squeeze the final days

of freedom, sunburns and sandcastles.
Farm boys finish chores early, ride bikes

to town, summer football drills.
When first I heard black tires squeal,

then, an awful thud, across our lawn, I ran.
Neighbors screamed me on, and when I saw

the boy, postured arms curled in, I knew.
Like a priest at his fount, our neighbor cradled

the child's torn head from the tar highway.
In a silent rage, teenage fists rose and sank.

I lifted his practice jersey, laid my ear to his chest,
counted his brave heart for a full minute, wondered

how he could yet breathe. From his pale lips, not
one whisper, (my nurse pockets, empty of any wand.)

Inside a white collar, we fixed his neck, strapped
him to a board, raised him to a gurney bed. Louder

than a soldier's widow, spinning lights wailed.
The wee song of his heart still taps within my head.

And I wished those sirens were red erasers
from Nickel's Five-and-Dime and my mother

was yet alive wearing Evening in Paris perfume,
her sleeveless lemon dress,
able to hold my hand all the way home.

BLUE MASON JAR

At the flea market my husband asks
Why'd you pick it up?
He's right, of course, when he reminds me

it holds no sailor's ship,
but just now cradled in both palms
a piece of August light

caught inside
and you saw your uncles
on Papaw's tractor

bare chested, young and tan.
Granny helps you fix
high noon's ice water.

Like a pony
you gallop toward them
both your hands full.

They smile, call you *honey*
say *please be careful*
then *thank you*

for a chance to rest,
a pause
carried to them in clean blue jars.

Soon, they will cross the crick,
mow the steep pasture,
their tractor on a slant.

Even now, you don't know why,
but you are afraid.

II.

To pray you open your whole self
To sky, to earth, to sun to moon
To one whole voice that is you.
And know there is more
That you can't see, can't hear,
Can't know except in moments
Steadily growing and in languages
That aren't always sound but other
Circles of motion.

—Joy Harjo
"Eagle Poem"

Doves Come to My Yard

These Amish ladies walk
in threes and twos, speak in coos.
Small skirts brush aside the fog.

I hear them reading Psalms,
leading sunrise service. Their
lame driver, his sorry white van

swallowed in morning's mist.
Across a fading lawn
doves spill like clover,

bonnets untied, gray wings
folded, a shawl over
each arm. Our kissed children?

Their village school bus? Long gone.

And chores start before dawn.
Under my pines, they gossip, whisper
near brown cones, choose

who'll fly first to my porch,
find my study's wide glass door.
Shy friends travel together. This

watched woman, her secret
piecing, so busy at her frame,
the heart's old order

weeping, teaching itself
how to wash stars, rinse lids,
ladle the doves' prayerful coos

sonnets in haunting stanzas
the low soft shadows of grief.

Breach Calf

The calf's hind feet point to barn rafters.
Inside his mama, he dreams a baby brother,

how they sit the moon's lap for a story.
Climbing down, he does a somersault, lands wrong.

And now, this farmer, his gloved arm pushes him
back and back and back, his mama strains at her plow.

Then, other rough men, special chains, metal wrapped
just below his knees, not wanting a cripple,

a calf who cannot run or play. Mama's fresh blood,
pain's awful hands squeeze, no breath for his whistle.

The beautiful boy asleep in clean straw,
but all in the manger are still,

save the bawling mother
washing her son, calling his name to the moon.

PLANTING PINES

Three pines stand, a row of royal
mamaws, tall in their velvet coats.

Their arms have lots of cots for robins,
empty cribs for wrens.

One Mother's Day, I asked for
a half dozen pines, Colorado blues,

a way to put a wall between cars
and my busy children chasing balls.

Even then, broad notebooks
thick with a monologue of worry.

The drought year, we nursed them,
carried bucket after bucket.

More babies squalling in the dark,
and we cannot hurry years. The trees

took a high school boy's four-door Ford
(his spine broken). Next, a college girl

spooked by a deer, full moon night
totaled her Chevy (she walked away).

My pines wept and coughed and burnt.
The iconic story of those spared? Well,

angels and gods take days off; women
know children trip, fall, get tied up

kicking inside the trunks of their lives.
Listen, you spot an abandoned car,

Please stop, remember me,
how I planted my trees.

LOCUST SHELL

Hanging sheets on the line,
you find a locust shell. It clings
to a pole's breast, one of two crosses
your husband cut, nailed and set thirty years ago.

Clean taste of clothespins in your mouth.

March winds, the poles brace themselves,
lean in, lean a little closer to the ground.
Suddenly, this dry well, a body outlined
in brown calls your hand to its brow.

What makes a woman take off, alone,
no note, no time to grab her coat?

In your palm, a tiny piano with no song,
gently, gently, you elevate her
thorax, the cave that held her heart.

Pressed against your chest,
a cupped hand tends the husk.
What fences do you pledge allegiance to?
What flag, this country?

Above sheets and aprons,
songbirds cast their spell, the sky's
metal blue lowers its faraway swing set.

Why not close both eyes, listen
for children's voices,
happiness blown from wands,
even cries from skinned knees?

Remember, forever,
the brief nature of light

with a kiss you'd heal the world.

PHOTO JOURNALIST

Like patio umbrellas our green tomatoes shade
these babies, six bunnies dressed in furry snowsuits.
God tells a joke in July, and quickly, you must run

for your camera. It's just this way, living out of town,
wanting a mess of fried green tomatoes for supper
(your grown daughter's favorite). Remember when

her small feet found those bees? And now, you stumble
on a new family moved into your garden overnight.
Their mother's gone to market after hours of labor,

her sweeping out years of someone else's dirt,
assigning beds inside the bunker. And it's hard work
getting six kids down for a nap. She's earned her coffee,

her sweet moment of rest after unloading all these boxes.
But see how the curtains fold back and she's propped
her kitchen door wide? Kneeling, peeping through leaves,

pressing your face against the nursery window, you feel
like a hospital cleaning lady. Soon, day turn nurses
will be back from lunch, and isn't it a little like sin

to photograph newborns? Faces down, butts stuck
high in the air, they cuddle together struggle to stay warm.
Don't be such a wuss, you tell yourself, *this is not to sell*

*—not even one copy—*but today, maybe God wants you
to understand juxtaposition, asks you to show a moving story,
not the one about a bush burning,

something easier,
a parable about hunger and blindness,
        how any life we find can make us full.

Swimming Hole

In the hayfield's corner, a rut
    fills every year. Spring
        rain blooms

its puddle, brown water hugged up
    by dirt. Days stacked,
        tied and bound,

tractor tires leave stories
    of great weight, much
        too heavy

for such soft ground. Generations
    of robins have found
        the sun's sink

and mirror, done shaving,
    now he shares.
        Uncles, aunts

cousins, the robins jump in
    laughing, splashing.
        Their happiness

a song. A bath without soap, a pool
    with no lifeguard. They dive
        and dive

into joy, wade under its spray,
    swallowing mouthfuls.
        Even babies

are not afraid
    orange vests
        protect them.

GOURD

The yellow skin has lost its shine.
One sundown, its patina floated up
like a ghost. Shaped like a weird fish
found by a springhouse, it never swam.

Holding it now, the blank face stares,
without eyes it studies me, has a swollen
pucker for its nose. Dried these many years,
it makes the sound of an infant's rattle
so rock it gently in your hands.

And given a chance, those seeds
might bear their flowers.
But, I'd have to hurt the gourd,
split it open, fillet it like a salmon.

It was a gift. My daughter's tall boyfriend,
an artist with deep blue eyes. Together,
they lived, laughed, cried, fought,
made up, made love. He said

she leaned into the warmth of his body
and told her nightmares. For a while
it helped her stand. And I love him for it.
Maybe this gourd's the baby
they tried so hard to make.

What skiff does hope resemble?
Why keep splinting its broken oar?
Kevin's ashes drift in her purse and dreams.
A shot glass swallowed him. Those last months,

people laughed, made fun of him riding his bicycle,
his drum belly, sad baskets of Wild Irish Rose.
But, aren't we all paddling the same raft?
the one called *ache and wonder*?

CORN ROWS IN AUTUMN

In slow moving lines
they shake, offer each other
the sign of peace,
watch for night,
sleep upright in wind boxes.

Acres of shaggy brothers,
they look down, shuffle
their shoeless feet,
sprung hair flung over foreheads,
jaundice eyes hidden.

Chapped hands, this big crew
where last year's hay grew, they
watch the next guy's back,
close attention paid
to dry coughs, any new raspy voice.

Not prophets, but aging hoboes adrift
Acme Corn, faded ink streams
stamped above shirt pockets.
No trains, lost crow tracks
littered with quail pennies.

Blue bandana sky and no campfire lifts
their shanty stories, shy as deer
with no legs to run.
Nothing shocks them, not baseball hail
or hoar frost, these gentle men
        eating empty cans of dreams.

OUR BACKYARD, LATE SEPTEMBER

I hear
ripe fellows

drop and cobbled
limbs thump

climbing over
feedlot rails. I go

to the sound
of night's hurt,

gathering my robe
close. I find

crawling shadows,
arms near broke.

Caught between
three maples

on his knees
the old moon

rubs dark carpet
a spectacle

he's lost
his hearing aid.

THE GARDEN IN WINTER

Row upon row,
snow waves

cover our garden.
In stiff trousers

the maple's shadow
walks his old dog.

Faint smell
of pipe tobacco

drifts behind them.
From his left pocket,

the man lifts a boy
like a timepiece, engraved,

something rare and precious,
a leaf's hand pressed in stone.

Shoveling nine steps,
I watch the puppet show.

With great effort
a twisted branch gets thrown,

the lab
makes a clumsy plunge.

In cold white sand
the boy runs, then whistles

to his friend.
Come back, come back

you're out too far;
(my toy heart lunges, gulps)

and I'm too winded to swim.

VIOLETS

Across our living room
they greet each other, wave slight arms.

Good women, these neighbors
who seldom visit, never carry tales.

Sunday afternoon,
buttoned sleeves rolled up, green blouses

pressed, long gray hair
twisted back, pinned in buns.

These Pentecostal sisters
come together, bring bouquets,

their small fists full of purple flowers,
married heads bowed down.

This morning
one of their young sisters passed.

Today, they will not be baptized in light
nor will they speak in tongues.

GLORY

A pink sky cradles our woods tonight
where October's trees become stained glass.
A restless river, this sky, though
you won't see John baptizing Jesus.
And across the center soy bean field
daylight rolls itself up, a parlor blind,
its failing hinge, a film shot in robin egg blue,
slate gray in patches, ashes needing shoveled
from a grate. And I think God is tired
of walking west, big bare feet fanning
His robe. He pauses, every third step,
to kiss shaky hands of leaves. Snow's
being spit, sweet dreamy flakes circle
the calves' pen, then run away.
Just now, lit by a dying sun, twin silos rise
like church spires. A hymnal's closing,
the broken fence, evening's gentle *Hallelujah*.

Both Shoes Off

You can barely remember it now.

Your mother holds a ball of yarn
passes its end to your fingers.

But where do girls go
pulling a pink clothesline?

You were thirsty.

Shimmering in the haze,
a guy with blue eyes, glasses.

His lips on your mouth
became a mountain stream.

You were someone else.

A woman lifting her daughter
from a highchair, a wife

hurrying to finish the lawn,
a new nurse giving shots.

You were happy there.

Being a mom, wiping cracker
mess in a dishcloth, smelling apples,

fresh sheets, letting go of your days
thrown breadcrumbs in the yard.

What was it like?

He was your song, your rainbow
parachute opening the thousandth time

your head against his warm shoulder,
dancing in the yellow kitchen,

slowly, with both shoes off.

BENEATH THE BIRD FEEDERS

Gray seeds, scattered corn
a broken rosary
in our hostas-matted hair.
Hail Marys, Our Father
answers unsaid prayer
to paint another spring.

THE WRENS

Walk knee deep in snow
brown cassocks drag the ground
breaking vows of silence.

Early April, Under the Crabapple Tree

Two blue-collared crows
a cardinal up from his chair
bitter wind hits each branch
aging nuns
swatting palms with a ruler
snow angels
singing Latin mass.

QUIETLY, DEEPLY

Beneath the ground
a river calls each leaf home.
Soft light above the sink,
a woman's hum,
her kitchen's open door.
One-by-one, we let go
maple branches, and we come.

III.

What we love, shapely and pure,
is not to be held,
but to be believed in.
And then they vanished,
into the unreachable distance.

—Mary Oliver
"Swans"

In this World

Where we are not gods,
but tenders of beautiful
and broken things

much depends on the woman
folding mountains
of warm socks, cleaning

small white shoes,
hiding colored eggs,
working for the dwarves.

GRAY WOOL CARPET

Smell of paint in the living room
of your new old house.

Your legs getting used to its floor
where a gray ocean floats bouquets,

deep rose flowers thrown overboard
long ago, some big ship bound for cities

you'll never see, its foreign port,
a white deck hemmed in fog. Paper confetti,

fur coat women wave to friends,
family on the shore. A champagne toast,

the ship's loud horn lifts the bow,
scatters blocks inside your home,

wrecks toy cars. A rag doll watches
your young face surprised now,

your two bare feet
splashing layers of petals,

dozens of roses just for you.

HOPE FOR WORDS

I am not Moses, but some mornings
asking a path to just *please* open,

I raise my pen over a white sea.
My two miracles? Turtle pancakes.

Snoopy dog houses built from snow.
Today, steering this flat sailboat,

I ran upon a sandbar made of words.
A woman swings shifts

like muddy loads won't round her shoulders,
like maybe she can bend the tides.

Dear reader, have you fished at sunset?
Do you recall pink mist and fog,

night's warm harbor sprinkled
with a hundred shrimpers' boats,

their small bright lights, cabin
lanterns blinking here and there?

Well, once, at a convenience store,
our son shouted *Beaver Eggs!*

His face aglow, like his cake's candles
lit and waiting. Barely six,

a tooth fairy dime in his shirt pocket,
lucky stones hug his shoebox whistle.

The sign said *Beverages.* We belly laughed
in our blue car. Amelia Earhart's lost,

but there are islands where no planes land,

shells of stories, pearls in dirt
underneath
      the world's quicksand.

First Dog

Our son's nine years old, facing fractions,
science projects, peewee football.

Without a brother fourth grade's a maze
of teachers, changing classes.

Beyond our budget, we buy a brindle pup
knowing shots cost money. We'll have to pay

to have her spayed. A silky boxer
wearing four white socks, on her chest

an arrow. Inside our weathered Chevy,
the puppy opens a child's cocoon.

In ten miles, she gets a hundred kisses,
he receives more, occasionally

she cries, shivers and shakes. Arms wide,
free falling. Our son feels her body's warmth

next to him, her heart beating. His hands comb
and pet. His arms circle her body.

Don't be afraid, he says,
(a voice of certainty I have never heard)

you're going home with me.
Across the front seat's tangled leash,

my husband squeezes my palm.
Yes, I think, looking as far as I can see,

*and wherever we are headed
        let no harm be.*

I HAVE ONLY A BROOM HANDLE

Inside our roof's wooly shaft,
a nest of babies, robins falling down.

From the dark choir loft,
a desperate symphony.

Our light's beam cannot lift
their grass raft past the chimney's ledge.

I have a wooden broom handle,
oily soot on both palms.

Mommy, I feel sorry for the birdies.
My daughter begs their freedom.

I draw her close, kiss her chestnut hair.
Why didn't they build their nest in our trees?

By half inches, we walk up cellar stairs.
We are just women waiting in our home

for a terrible silence that will surely come.

WHEN YOU'RE THIRTY-EIGHT

Wheels under us, the good earth turns,
and your daughter's eyes when she asks,
Mom, can we go skating? It's a big deal
in the second grade, and her cheek's curve,
an eclipse. How to tell her I can't skate.

At thirty-eight, failure
tastes like bonbons in your lap
while you're watching afternoon soaps.
So fearing failure, you pile four gigglers

into your yellow hatchback and fake it.
The oak floor's a paddle on your butt
and knees. The silver ball twirls and laughs
in color when you drop. Only the snack

bar is friendly, hot dogs spin on carousels,
one-armed pretzels smile under white freckles
and popcorn blows its warm breath against
a window. Knowing you can't always hold

her hand, you draw back, tighten brown
laces, give her a hug and a push. After each
spill, her body rises, a foal on ice. Her hokey-pokey
face grins. In a butterfly net, isn't she

your finest dream? She wobbles, leans
scrawny ponytails into the springtime shoulder
of her own wind. Watching her, you realize
it's not the planked oak that crushed your wings,

not the flat out falls that bent your antennae.
It was the silent, endless, hypnotic waving
of tiny white flags.

HOMEROOM POET-MOM:
FOR THE SECOND GRADERS, CATHOLIC ELEMENTARY 1989

I did it because Sister Marilyn said I could,
because we both saw
the blindness of Pac Man,
the quiet lesson of eating others
who don't look like us.

I did it because after we learn the letters,
someday somebody writes F on our paper.
Because when they don't get our pink trees
with blue apples, they'll point and giggle.
Mom, you hung my Mayflower upside down.

For voice I did it, because one day I knew
they'd be called upon to right world mistakes.
I did it because I knew the magic sweet potato
rooting its vine in water
was a Band-Aid on childhood's sinking ship,

and by the time we see the iceberg,
well, you know the rest. I did it because
Stephanie's mom *has hair like brown shoelaces*,
Kevin's grandpa's kiss *tastes like a popsicle*,
and when Brandy's dad hugs her *I feel*

like I'm flying. I did it so when the big grid fails,
the power's out, they'd be able to find the way
to their own cupboards, feed themselves and others
with whatever wheat's in the pantry. I did it because
not everybody lives at Ozzie and Harriet's, and

(at least in second grade) policemen can *be our friends.*
I did it because we are paper dolls,
terrible and wonderful hands bend us
then throw us away. I did it because
that's my daughter chewing her pencil in row three

and in a creek, my feet sink.
As an act of contrition, I did it
for all the sins of my life.

54

THOSE BOYS WHO WERE FOURTEEN

sank against locker room walls after basketball practice,
saw the fight, heard who started it, knew who threw

first punch, but it was our son in the ER getting
his forehead stitched on Saturday night.

And when I went to his coach, hat in hand,
begging another chance, he told me

all about *the rules*, how both boys were off
the Tiger team, but he'd go to the others, who had

years ahead of them to grow into lanky feet,
get rid of their teeth's braces. If a single pimply

face would say it was not the fault of our son,
he'd let him back on the team. *I don't hold out*

much hope, he said handing me his hanky,
they're only fourteen. Never offer your tears

to a man without hope, he knows his characters,
spiders they like to kill, the ones who'll laugh

when a wing's pulled off a butterfly. My son came
to supper, couldn't eat, left his jersey, sneakers,

jock strap on his dresser like a shrine. The sutures
once lifted, left a small scar, but silver number ten

flashed its hill's broken mirror for months
when I made his bed. When the coach called, his

voice cracked asking the uniform be returned.
The other boy? Had baseball, football, the lead

in the freshman play. *Never rinse off your hoe*
before the garden's done. There's still time.

I believe somebody wants to come clean.
Wherever you are, call me collect,
    I'll come, your house or mine.

LESSONS IN GRAVITY:
HIGH SCHOOL PHYSICS PROJECT

A light in our cellar where cobwebs
are sashes holding rafters. A stained
workbench near the utility sink,
a paper nest: the physics teacher's
instruction sheets.

A man, a girl building a model bridge,
drunk with purpose, they measure, cut
and glue. They inhale and exhale, ten
thousand breaths. Smell of kerosene rags.

A furnace coughs, warms our yellow house.
How to think in terms of math and pressure.
The man's a potter singing the clay's
potential to his daughter.

In the kitchen, I stand alone, stirring
at my stove: salty circles of celery, chicken,
carrots. Water carries floating bodies of noodles.
Mistakes are part of discovery, and this time

next week we will learn the wrong wood
was sold to our daughter for the bridge: bass
not balsa. She will say, *The bridge held
thirty-two pounds before breaking. I got an F*

because bass is stronger than balsa.
Listen, there's no end to the epic of everyday life,
the height of hope, the yoke of stories and scribes.
See, how my arm becomes a lever,
pushes this stick through her ashes?

BACKYARD PIETA:
DEATH OF THE FAMILY DOG

Spike grew feeble, crippled, fit
only for tail wagging. He whined,
we carried fresh water, always,
a clean bowl, we held dog haunches
with our hands so he'd stand, swallow
softened grain pellets. We carted him
down and up the steps—night
and day and night—the need to move
his bowels, relieve his bladder.

The alphabet of love is *come, shake, sit, stay,*
a pillow between soul and ground.
Finally, the strain and heave of his boxer
chest and front paws dragging the bent sled
of his fawn backside was unbearable—
I went to a vet, hired his hemlock.
My husband dug and dug the earth's
cool brown cot. Eleven years
of chewed slippers, wrestled sticks,
puppy smell in our daughter's bed.

Backyards become murals, patchwork
years filled with picnics, piñatas,
shy candles of fireflies, timid snowmen
with crooked smiles dying in the sun.
This father leans on his shovel, cries,
understands plea and indictment, Mary's face
in our daughter's eyes,
how she sits, cradles her dog, gentles him
to her chest as the vet's needle enters us all.

WHEN THE FURNACE MEN TAKE OUR OIL TANK

Six of them came, good workers, men
the napes of clean necks in cotton shirts.

Smell of cigarettes and aging grease,
tough hands of fathers with rope blue veins.

At our cellar's far end, all these years
(and they've been many) the tank stood alone.

Painted tractor green, four haunches on legs,
a gauge on top like a whale's blowhole.

The freak of the house, covered with dust
our kids wrote letters on its hide.

From the bowl of its paunch not one groan,
never a belly ache. Only once, we lost heat,

when we were busy being dumb and young
we let it run dry. Back then sixty-nine cents

bought a gallon of oil. We got a new mule
geothermal, heats, cools. Like pallbearers,

furnace men lift and wrestle the oil tank.
A green fat man, his first time up the stairs.

Legs stiff, head first, thighs open to air
bright sun strikes like a welder's flash.

Not one tear, not one moan.
Gone, our metal canvas and its artists' names.

Every Star You Behold:
A Letter from the Mother

I pray we appear as two
white butterflies
in your yards
on days when trouble rises
like water in a cellar,
like a barn full of blackbirds.

When you see us humming
in gauzy shawls, shopping
without money, rain's voice
is your father, my words are wind.
And in the time of little honey,

slowly find your holy spot,
the choir of a hidden pond,
the meadow's canvas.
Go there and empty anger,
open your heart's bloody fists,

rip the ledger's every page.
Be mindful of violets
and frogs. Stay through dusk,
over the campfire's smoke,
let night's velvet come down.

Every star you behold?
Mistakes we can never take back.
Love's the oldest rope,
hold tight its hemp and throw
it across the sky, keep walking
on it, forgive everyone,
even yourself.

IV.

And I wonder about
this lifetime with myself,
this dream I'm living,
I could eat the sky
like an apple
but I'd rather
ask the first star
why am I here?
why do I live in this house?
who's responsible?
eh?

—Anne Sexton
"The Fury of Sunsets"

HOW WE LEARN TO THROW THE DICE

Cheyenne Bodie, Maverick, Bonanza's Little Joe.
What ten-year-old girl didn't love cowboys?
Couldn't feel herself pressed against Joe's

waist flying on his paint pony? I swore to be
Miss Kitty, fall in love, never marry.
But then, a blue-eyed guy with thick glasses:

one kiss, I caved. We wanted the whole show,
saw the Cape Cod, a small house full of work
no porches, no sidewalks, doors without steps.

How do folks get in? How do they get out?
Night's pale lights, people inside are dealing
with summer's heat, window fans spinning.

FOR SALE sign, red and white as a child's
kite propped near a sugar maple extends
gray limbs, says *Take a chance on me.*

A ladder leans north, its handyman gone,
his fresh coat of white newly trimmed.
Around each pane, black primer grins,

catches my eye like a nun in a tattoo parlor
making the sign of the cross before she exposes
her deltoid, unites ink and flesh. I write numbers,

get lucky when I call. The realtor opens wide
a saggy back door. We enter a house full of sleep.
In her chair, a grandmother pretends to sew.

She makes no sound when the salesman grabs
a glass. *Taste this water; it's from a spring.*
When I leave them, the guy has my husband

drinking, his fingers tap a table asking for cards.
Azure haze filters through the air like smoke.
My beautiful cowboy and this carpetbagger

with papers selling him a lot
      telling him how he'll spend his life.

PAINTING THE HOUSE

The air spoke fall and we hurried
to choose a color unlike any house

either side of the road. Sears
had an end-of-season sale, a man

who looked like my dead high school
principal figured the gallons for two coats.

Smoke blue trimmed in white, the colors
of a gathering storm. Up and down

borrowed ladders, we learned to march,
reshaped coat hangers, bent dark metal

so they'd serve us, hang our paint
from wooden rungs, hold those gallon cans,

save our palms the painful crease.
Scraping's the worst. Chips scratch your eyes,

back and forth, over and over the wire brush
bristles like a boy who hides from chores.

And you can't blame him; it's July,
so darn hot an egg may fry on your legs,

salty sweat runs, eyebrows to pupils.
All you want is to wade a crick, take off

on your bike, but the house grabs your elbow
firmly as a mean teacher, to let you know

*Homework must get done. How else
will you grow up? Amount to something?*

Smoke blue paint splashes your forearms,
speckles your face, even streaks your hair

making it gray. Now, holding
your own hands, walking backwards

in the mist, you stare at your painting,
the dream they said you'd want.

NEW ROOF
for Uncle Gerald

Men crawl on our roof like ants opening peonies.

Near the gable my uncle steadies a level,
measures how much fall there is in a foot.
Built between wars, ours is a steep pitch,
this house, a woman showing her age.

He helps my husband do the math
for bundles, our new brown roof.
His yellow pencil draws a pattern
and piles of aching arms. Dear reader,

you may not know shingles' first rows
go upside down. Both of us are so green
we might be leprechauns or new hires from Mars.
For roofing, grab ladders, scaffolding,

lots of coffee (black), youth's strong back.
You may pray to them, but roof fairies
will not fly over, will not lift shingles at night,
nor will they sew my uncle's thumb.

It starts to rain, in the distance, thunder.

My uncle, a Korean vet, has a full-time life,
a house, two girls, a wife. Still, he steers
my husband, his wheel of friends. Labor
without pay, ruined shirts, jeans never
again to come clean, burgers in tar-stained hands.

Merciless sun. Merciless sun.
Breeze, where are you? Sleep, please come.
Higher than flagpoles these men work without nets.
Fear opens my chest, yellow birds fly.

The roof drains our sweetness, like a salesman
hangs around longer than he should. I keep
hot coffee coming, remember to ice the beer.
Final row, the cap's cut, fit to the withers, pairs

of thighs burn squeezing its ribs, and then
the men ride our house like a horse in the sky.
Merciless sun, cover your eyes.

FROZEN PIPES, DECEMBER 1976

If you know a plumber, shake
his hand. Who else willingly
wades through crap, fishes
for tampons and toy cars?

See my kitchen, the man I love
half swallowed under the sink?
His blue jeans mended (both knees),
those careful patches? Mine.

A die setter, all his knuckles
stay boogered up. He's no surgeon
but watch, just now his open palm
begs a pipe wrench.

I've kissed every greasy line.
Listen, December's wind
found our key under a mat,
let himself in. Kitchen sink, bath tub

drains frozen, icy fists. In a sea
of rags, sack potatoes and oven cleaner
I kneel. Plumbing is holy work. Look,
my husband holds his blowtorch,

blue flame close as a kiss to his face,
he does not burn. Water drips through
layered newspapers, none of us drown.
Darkness twists his arms, they bend,

they do not break. Breathing smoky fumes
like incense, kids cry for a drink,
our dog barks, crazy over the flame.
I continue to kneel, believe completely

in the brotherhood of plumbers.
We both know heaven sent this wind,
the pipe wrench slips again,
and *Jesus Christ* is called upon.

WHEN MY BROTHER'S HOUSE BURNED TO THE GROUND

One morning as I knelt
on the floor of my kitchen
alone, humming
in the good-bones church
that is myself,
I placed my head inside the stove's oven,
scrubbing runaway blood
of burnt blackberry pies.
And a sweet voice said, *Rise up,*
call your brother in West Virginia,
tell him to bring his whole family
here, to Ohio, for Thanksgiving.
The voice felt like a field of soft fog.
(Mother bent over her wringer
washer, its tub full of dirty diapers.)
So I knew to shuck my yellow gloves,
go straight to the phone.
Ben and his family made the journey.
Three hours in a borrowed car,
snow drifts, ice and wind. His pretty wife
mashed potatoes. We floated
inside warm steam, rooms alive
with common stars,
our dog chasing balls and wells
of children's laughter. Family
bellies swollen with turkey
and too much pie. We fell asleep.
Night's phone rang. It put
its gun to our temples,
each call was an awful knell.
Our dreams crushed by bad news.
Ben's house afire, burning, gone!
My brother's face: Ulysses',
his mind's eye sifts layered ashes.
Where's a tapestry that spells HOME?
We held each other, wept and wept.
Ben, his wife and son were saved.
And our Mother's voice was not dead,
but an ocean's breaking wave
coming back and back and back.

MOMENTS IN THE KITCHEN

A metal rack, black cake cooling.
Here, where we've carved pumpkins and turkeys,
torn foil and bent forks, broken glasses
and promises, I stand ironing flannel sleeves.

The phone rings, my husband answers,
Yes, yes, I remember you Mike, (his old union
president), the pipe factory, closed.
Dave, how many are left?

In any holy city, it seems wrong to kick ruins,
even to read the tomb's roster. Seven years
my husband labored and cut, mixed and loaded
asbestos pipe, after Berlin's Crisis, prior to the end

of Agent Orange. Years before OSHA's filtration masks,
crews ripped sacks, emptied fibers into vats:
"African Blue" and "Canadian Blush."
Don't those names make you think exotic birds?

A warm shot of birthday bourbon? Cauldrons
of asbestos shavings, water and cement stirred,
slurry of gray soup poured over a screened
drum and felt cloth, oven dried like bread,

then, both ends lathed for water or sewage lines.
Cancer's a witch, her satchels and spells, a talcum
they breathed, salts they bathed in shift upon shift.
I packed his lunch, kissed him goodbye.

Outside, frost left its handprint on our maple.
Doesn't autumn break your heart: windy violins,
street-dancing leaves and constant confetti?
Winter? There's no way to stop it.

I mean my husband spoke the names of the dead
and a dozen hungry boys sat at our table
begging chocolate cake.

KITCHEN CUPBOARDS

You have a plan, a scheme
of colors for elderly faces, one
by one, doors lie supine, patterns

of lines emerge like scars.
Digging its own trench
the router's bit chews and spits.

Stripped of its covers
your kitchen shivers, wide-eyed
spices, bright blue cups.

A haunting village, its silent voices,
a sea of faces from every hut.
On Sunday's paper, you paint

your doors: yellow, peach, white,
left hand steadies the right.
Near the quart can stories of starvation,

another war, some soccer field,
a woman stoned to death. You have
a plan. Dip your brush, from the horsehair

press the excess, keep breathing,
keep painting. Your little cough?
Sounds like you're choking? *Sawdust.*

The throbbing headache? *Fumes.*
Aren't you too old to run naked,
screaming in desert streets?

Dip your brush, from the horsehair
press the excess, (six more doors)
keep breathing, keep painting.

The way it is
later today or tomorrow night
the doors will finally be dry,

you and your husband can hang them
then, with the other missionaries,
you'll be free to leave.

Washed Stone Delivery, Wrong Day, 1978

Our soles burn with arthritis,
so it's not a stretch to think of Fred
Flintstone, how he used to power
his boulder car with pudgy toes.

I'm not Fred's wife, still we
were mindful of dollars when
we ordered two ton of washed stone,
no less, no more (me in college,

two cars, the house). An extra rock
might just sink us. For delivery
we said, *Tuesday, after three PM.*
The next Monday after Chemistry I,

my husband's third ten-hour shift
kids with science projects, strep throat,
we found a mountain of river stones
drifted and settled down, like a man

in a hammock, napping in our driveway.
A mystery, no bill stuck to our door or
stuffed in the mailbox, and even for five treats
we could not make our dog talk.

To figure the mix-up, my husband called
our farmer neighbor. *They came, I guess
around two. They'd unloaded
by the time they found me,*

came right into the barn, he laughed.
Hey, don't worry, I wrote 'em a check.
He was gloved, worming his cows,
pushing pills into wet mouths.

The delivery men? Were young, poor.
And inside stables, what's one more
miracle? Ask the twin calves, kittens
scaling a ladder to the loft, our angel

neighbor whose boots smell of dung.

My Husband Was in a Hospital Bed

for six weeks, lost forty-two pounds,
a thousand razors skinning him inside,

on-fire pain, his left buttocks to foot.
If he were a horse, you'd put him down.

Six doctors scratched their heads
ordered more x-rays, every fancy test.

He had his best friend saw his shot gun
off. Three times a day I called crying

to the nurse practitioner, *He's lost eight
more pounds.* "I'll tell the doctor," was all

she said. He couldn't sit. He could not sit.
Do you know what that means?

For your body to not be able to bend?
Eating at the table with your family? Done.

Winter's bitter mornings, we'd have to
get him lifted up, jockeyed down nine icy steps

to a warm ambulance. The men would come:
Sonny, Joe, Arvie, Bob, Ron and Stew,

three for each side of the gurney.
I'd stand in my kitchen, hold the door

while backs divided his weight, black and white
hands together on metal bars, carnival guys

snapping couples in Ferris wheel seats,
brothers lifting a picnic table, gusts of wind

mussed their hair. Men will not tell you how
cold the river is nor how dark, but their arms,

just call them miracle's boat. They rowed us
to Hell's other side, where my husband got well.

WHEN THE STEERS GOT OUT OF THE BARNYARD

After his first visit to Chicago's meat packing plants,
Henry Ford formulated plans for the assembly line.
                              —PBS documentary

We didn't know our neighbor's milk maid
had quit due to advanced kidney disease.

We didn't see it was just him, his wife
for three shifts of milking, tending four kids

(two in diapers.) We didn't know anything
but to try and head the snorting beasts back

one morning, waving pitiful twigs, branches
like wands to shoo bad steers into their pen.

Hooves sucking divots from Andy's manicured
yard, super-sized tongues picking Helen's cherry

tomatoes, munching Judy's green peppers.
My husband found rotted posts they'd leaned

and shouldered all their weight against, slack
barbed walls, mud floors spooned through.

Who knew steers liked tossed salads
for Sunday brunch? We barely knew steer

from cow, and if I tell you now, the truth,
that from the black and white gang, not one made it

to the highway's ditch, will you be glad?

Dusk

Late May and behind our houses
a road lies, the gravel suffers
a patch of skin altered by its rash,
scarred spine, years of combined ruts.
Aging fence lines pasture windswept grass.
Retired die setter, my husband's
the patron saint of teacup roses and dirt.

Dusk and our farmer neighbor slows
his tractor, over its drone he talks and listens
(two hundred acres scream his name.)
My husband leans on a gray fender, his
bent fingers laced (twice in one week
he's planted peppers, tomatoes, beans.)
A late frost came, now both men speak
the lysis of hurts, balm to quiet them.

My husband's heart stents (all four) pale,
spent, never miss their wet tunnel's shift.
Richard's sixty cows bawling in stalls,
beg to be milked. Field mice,
the big barn, drifting voices of men,
their words the murmur of bees inside the hive,
a hammer's long sigh between nails.

Winter in the Township

The stillness of my country
we think

it's just us against elements.

Lighting oil lamps we barely speak,
we smother

what we cannot bear to see.

Tonight's plows driven by men
will open the soft belly of darkness,

press what falls deep into a ditch.

All this work, all this white
and much weight gathers on the striped mattress.

We fail and fall asleep,

old lovers inside the curves. Old lovers missing
their young life. Up and down both lanes,

trouble over and over,

broken necks of mailboxes, red arms flailing.
Some sort of code or alarm?

A letter our brothers and sisters
cannot write? A message that cannot wait?

Elders, children and moms
fathers and sons, villages bombed,

a billion-trillion dreams fall to earth
like confetti, like snow.

Gone, gone the ancient temples' songs,
brown arms, scarves and bracelets sailing.

PAPER

What if the body's a curve of circles hidden in a trunk,

never knowing if lightning will strike, split us in two,

no way to predict the next ice storm followed by bitter winds,

a force ripping off arms, leave us oozing sap?

Born lucky, we might be a Sequoia, live a long time.

Maybe people in Congress like old stuff, so for a while,

we seem protected, still, in dreams, the sounds of saws

the axe blade's toothless grin. And when it comes

surely there will be options on the other side, changed

into a dining room table, families gather round us to eat,

children erasing fractions spill hot cocoa, carved

roasts, gravy ladled on bread. Or, we might go through

a chipper, get mixed with goop, become pressed boards

they sell for stalls, our pulp sent off to paper mills.

And if our story begins, *Once I was a tree in a lovely forest,*

it's not so bad to end up here as the heart's raft holding

what is precious in our lap, rocking it back and forth,

humming lullabies to this letter we wrote then folded,

a note we pulled from a burning house, the wadded draft

thrown out with trash we've saved and taped to a wall,

a life better than millions of others and not to be wasted.

V.

Surely the earth can be saved
by all the people
who insist
on love.

Surely the earth can be saved for us.
—Alice Walker
"These Days"

SNOW MOUNTAINS BY THE GARAGE

Weeds around my neighbor's pond are peasants
driven from their village. Brown heads down,
they shiver, shuffle to a new mountain range
near our garage. My neighbor's plow left a ragged

row of blue snow. Fathers grumble, mothers' scarves
blow, babies chew their fists. Ten days since my surgery,
I'm the old bear hugging herself in our cave. I let the Sherpa
wind come in, hang his coat on a wall. He will sit and listen,

what he hears, he'll never tell. Bone counting is not easy,
never quick. White waves drift over steps, ice prisms sparkle
from eaves. Maybe our house is a chandelier dropped
in a hayfield. Legions of bird tracks cross the yard, so

my husband dons his boots, carries seed and suet. Wrens,
cardinals, lost in his breath. The vulnerable must be fed,
and yesterday, he knelt, bandaged our mailbox's broken neck.
Me? I'm not fit to drive nor lift more than a sack of sugar.

Sweet. I tend the good fireplace, burn endless logs
of nothing, and I have a chair, my pen, warm tea.
Tree branches shiver like bells, but no church hides us.
Someone must write for the wounded, wave homeless boys

inside for soup. We have no priest, but just now,
the moon passes for a wafer, no, a flashlight.
Sky trauma. God's been found in a snow bank.
Peter's cut off His coat, a trillion goose feathers fly.

This blizzard makes the barn disappear. In heaven,
Mary wipes His face with her towel, Martha piles
on steamy blankets. And in the south pasture,
a woman wearing a babushka folds a note:

We were here, babies nursed, no beds.
Snow mountains by the garage. Really.
And if you're reading this, it's spring,
yellow tulips have risen,
        and our mountains are surely dead.

WE HAVE STARTED TO GIVE OUR STUFF AWAY

The scarred highchair,
odd dishes, a lantern bought
for camp, and now, my uterus.

Oh Lord of dirt floors, tent
flaps undone by time's wind,
I toss prom's mauve purse,

its red trail of dreams, empty as a pail
fallen from its shelf. My garage sale,
my self without a sign. I'm on display,

the hood's up, and my lady doctor
flashes a light, shakes her head.
My stuff huddles under a frayed

coat, shot doves caught in a barrel
of wet leaves. Her ceiling's a white sail,
my ovaries, twin boats. Without stars,

with no moon, sixty years to row me here.
We discuss clots, robotics, knives
fit to cut bruised pears. *Please*

bear down, she says, then sighs.
Well, your prolapse is a four.
What? I'm not a ten? Lady, (I want to say)

you just entered THE LOVE SHACK.
Can't you read my thighs' marquee?
Move your speculum to the right.

Now, can you palpate a peace sign?
Find the torn poster of Sonny & Cher?
The back stage painting of my sixteen-year-old breasts?

Yes, that hurts. Did you know? My sweetheart
went to Vietnam. A long tangled web of lies,
a world of puppets, strings, and small town guys.

In boxes boys came home to mothers, wives
—a sadness we cannot know—
to be young and done with our lives.

At the Heart Doctor's Office, I Take the Last Seat

Midmorning, leather chairs the color of crushed grapes,
my husband's first check-up after his fourth stent.

Musty smell of a grandfather's sweater, a woman
digs a Kleenex from her walker's bingo apron.

The only thing missing is a yawning cat. I grab
a seat by a young couple, their dreaming newborn

and the all-legs, antsy child beside them. Her chatter's
like spilled marbles, *School starts this week.* I ask her age

and grade. Her daddy's name is called, his woman's eyes beg.
I nod yes, just leave her here. We both know the next room's

a broom closet and her man's ashy as a cellar mop.
The pretty nurse closes her door and four souls vanish.

The pixy girl says, *Daddy needs a new heart, for his heart
attack was really big.* (She draws a circle with twig arms).

*And did you see Mommy's picture in the paper? Yesterday.
Page one, between her brothers. They robbed the donut place*

*where she works. Now they're in jail, and I live with Daddy
and Janie.* My husband sits by the window, his hands folded.

Is that your baby sister? *Oh yeah, that's Susie. And Janie,
she did not know the baby was getting born. She thought*

she was peeing her pants. What's in your sack?
A children's book I wrote. Would you like to see it?

You wrote a book? Yes. I'm taking copies to the library.
Hmm, baby turtles dancing with their shells, but is the turtle

really marrying a mouse? Yes. *Well, did you paint the pictures?*
No, I have a friend. She's an artist. *I have a dog, but not no more.*

See, my flip-flop's broke right here. Her auburn braids shine;
freckles pepper her nose. *I am just done with second grade.*

Why do you wear those big shoes? Don't you like flip-flops?
She coughs, and it's the phlegm of black dust.

I remember her father's rumpled hair, Janie's slack
belly slung over gapped jeans, the baby, how they

reappeared looking like they'd fallen down a well.
I might have taken the girl like sack candy from its shelf,

bought her blue paints and clay, read her stories,
watched her play, but somewhere she has a dog,

and it will rub its neck raw tugging chains,
it will bark for her every night.

LIFE FLIGHT

I am a cloud drifting past a window where I was first a nurse.
avalanche of bodies bound in cotton, ceiling lights raining down.
Decades since I've run those stairs, steered my medcine cart
and its paper sails, tickets naming the sick,
up the reef of beige halls.

I have rainbow pills, water from a jug, syringes, needles
kept in shallow drawers. I am here to help the heart's fist
squeeze and twist its red mop. Pain is a forest. My hands?
Both ends of a two-man saw, my will, its blade.

I want to feel the knot of fear again as I did then,
mixing an insulin drip, holding Dig when the apical
was a lazy turtle, counting stacked breaths,
pushing morphine slowly, slow.

I want to be star-struck again
—my afternoon charge nurse wearing her owl glasses
caught that mousey lady, carried her, like a ragdoll
safely to bed—I want to comb Mrs. Byrd's puff
of white hair, smooth her muslin gown's gauzy blue.

I want to be liquid as the doe I was then.
I want the moon to be a newborn,
her life's at risk, and I'm the flight nurse. Down
the hall of gypsy nights, I am the steady wren.

I'm the one who brings her to her mother's arms.
I'm the one who sings her sweet face home.

MILKWEED

When I tell my husband we need to plant it
he tells me *Honey, it's just a weed* and *Where*

would we sow it? Already, most of the bees
are gone, queens race around hives

like their hair is on fire. Forests are auctioned
off like slaves, and when I tell him the monarch

butterflies are dwindling, milkweed's the only
place they lay their eggs, he sits down to read.

All around us, chemicals burst seams of gas,
aneurysms blow, wells hemorrhage.

Another loaded gun's pressed to Blair Mountain's
soft temple in southern West Virginia.

In Nigeria, men with machetes and grenades, an all
girls' school, children taken alive to kneel in hell.

Wisdom, mercy, love.
There must be seed,
  but where's the ground to grow it?

CARRY ON

You stand in line, both shoes off,
all the days of your life folded, packed.

Like a long-necked bird you squint
to read departure times.

How long is the flight, Mom?
Children's voices pale as cream,

soft as sugar. *Hold hands, stay together,*
you say. You tighten her ponytail, wipe

his nose. They will have to fly over
the most open part of the sea

and turbulence kinks everyday weather.
You weave them through waiting rooms

of chairs, show them how seats empty and fill.
Some pews lit with faith, others scarred

by courage. But were they listening?
All those nights of picture books—

the one where mountain heather blooms
and sings the rabbit to a high place, where he stops

the sacrifice of oxen? Soon, you may be called
to your gate, no telling how fast you'll have to run.

Everything Becomes A Mirror

The power company
has a plan
for our old maple's
wild bushy dreds,
her weathered arms
flagging trucks down.

TELL ME WHAT ELSE I SHOULD HAVE DONE

My morning
to drag the trash can back
when I saw a piece of you
lying prone, bloodless
chunk of maple
half wrapped in a veil of snow.

Straight away
I left the blue handle,
flew to your apron's shade,
gathered your angled branch
careful as a newborn
to my chest. Old friend,
I am sorry for the wind's

butcher block, his deep howl
last night. Here we stand
our best days spent, hours
borrowed like sugar, no plan,
forty years gone, limping along
aging bones, this rolling pin
limb, twisted, broken off.

Pain? Well, we don't know.
And doesn't our lawn's snow
remind you of sack flour?
Every fall counts,
and the hour to sew your
arm? Gone. I'm no sleuth,
but there was ample evidence
of struggle, aft and ahead,

gray flesh spiraled. Sister,
accept the shelter of my barn
coat's red, a warm space inches
from my heart, and I will pen
the note you can never write
for me: *Inside the fire ring,*
I waited for spring.
A woman carried me.
I was the eldest tree
wed to our front yard,
the end was sweet, not hard.

HERE AND ELSEWHERE

Ah, the finches return today confused.
They didn't witness our ladder's crash against
hooked feeders, my husband's near fall.

All they know is hunger, how they want to eat.
We live on a busy, busy street, a mile past the marsh
deer, snapping turtles, no antennae for trucks.

Like us, critters have their work, no vote
about paved roads splitting their turf. Sweet meat
in the turtle's shell tastes like chicken fixed with rice

or boiled for soup. Each day my husband takes our boxer
in his truck, buys coffee, newspapers, the Mighty Mart
in town. One Tuesday full of fog, he spots a turtle schlepping

toward the double yellow lines. Like a cop, my husband whips
around, stops traffic (both ways), grabs the old fellow's tail.
The turtle squirms, snaps, tries his best to bite

before my husband plops him into the bog. A Harley rider leads
applause, my husband waves, drivers clap, the banker,his son
sullen in new tattoos, the grandma with her yappy mutt.

Deep in the swamp, the turtle slept or kept marching.
I didn't know I married El Cid, and for her silence, our dog
got an extra treat. Look at my blistered palms. To carry

a story's hard, and for lots of reasons I almost didn't tell.
A turtle's wisdom, not to trust the first hand out,
aid to help a guy travel where he's bound.

Tomorrow and tomorrow and tomorrow, semis,
the approaching tanks, yellow birds
the precious little one man can do.

PRAYER FOR MY VILLAGE

That we may all live to see
where God drives His hot pink go-cart,

some piece of land facing both hills,
an ocean sunset, banana muffins cooling

on a sill. A cove where we are busy in shifts
building a platform, digging deep

and drinking from one gourd.
A plaza where our children sing in a classroom

and papers are not graded by degrees.
A schoolhouse where we all pass.

That we may dance in those streets
even for one just day,

the sweet pulp of happiness
bubbling up, swirling

so high, we must wear galoshes.

KILLDEER

Tan river stones edge our small yellow house,
four brown speckled eggs, inches from the driveway.
Before she gave into the nest, debates were fierce,
came daily, it was both-arms-up-revival-preacher-passion,
first the female and then the male, followed by both.

Warmer days, you lock down screens, don't plan
to eavesdrop, but things happen, a breeze carries
voices in. I mean homesteading in stones? Only two
for such a risky crater? So many rocks to be rolled back,
and it's work to rake ground, their antsy feet, their legs

thin as wires, but tough enough to clear a lot,
create a spot for temporary housing. Well into night
there was much discussion about traffic patterns—
my tan car, the mailman's van, my husband's red truck—
tires scatter gravel, pass too close to this new cottage.

She screams at him, *What were you thinking?*
Our babies will never make it from here to the fields.
In a huff, she turns around. He struts toward her.
Did you see the neighbor's combine? he shouts back.
The female drags her left wing like it's breaking,

wrings her hands, cries. Their parent eyes pierce and beep
a radar fixed on us, and they seem to never sleep,
these two spitfires whose mission is fly, feed, fret.
They watch my husband sharpen his lawnmower's blade,
see me hang baskets of blood red begonias, bury vines,

smell smoke from fall leaves. Tomorrow, we'll lower
the porch swing, wash winter off her wrinkled face,
fetch floral glider cushions from our cellar,
but not in a rush, not in a hurry. Our forty-third year;
slowly, slowly we welcome summer as our guest.

The killdeer? They are newlyweds fussing
about paint colors and who tracked mud on the rug.
And the children who'll run next across this lawn?
They are not our worry.

TURQUOISE

When a cow dies, the farmer hooks
his chain 'round a hind leg.
A thousand pounds of Holstein
gets dragged
way out yonder to the fields.

Number 417 took sick, May 19 died.
The farmer's logbook shows,
with a herd, selling milk, there are rules.

For no reason, I think of Brazil, where
my professor's wife was born.
He told us rancheros, servant families,
in a census were not counted.
*When they die, their passing, like their birth,
is no more than a cow's tail flicking a fly.*

Even now cow 417 studies the sky's
blue, the color of a woman's
turquoise skirt, a woman who shoos
chickens back, opens her door
across a dirt floor.

Her hair shines black as her skillet.
Maybe she motions us to her table.

Dear reader, from your soft chair
please rise,
enter her sinkless kitchen,
hold hands with her flickering life
let us count ourselves, *one, two, three*
before we pray, before we eat.

BARNS PAINTED WITH QUILT SQUARES

On country roads or near busy freeways
they surprise you, shoulders of wide gray barns
brought back to life, aging church women
given an autumn corsage, bright orange-yellow-
blue-red-greens rest on their bosoms.

Wanting to honor her mother's life and art,
my friend, a woman, started this painting.
Her mother's a *master quilter* which means
she sees bolts of cloth the way Leonardo
saw marble. Her scissors free squares of gingham,
triangles of feedsack, strips of calico.

Like evening porch talk, patches get sewn together.
To quilt, you must sit still, be responsible
for color choices. You will prick your fingers,
bleed and create a mess. All of this falls into your lap,
well, sometimes you think it's just too much.

The figuring out part never ends, after those squares
join hands, there's the batting and making do
for the quilt's back. Folded up in your dresser's
bottom drawer, years of scraps wave their arms.
Why not me? They seem to beg. It amazes you
fitting rows together, the simple grace of a choir.

How certain hymns raise your eyes to blue sky
like those barns and their lone star postage stamps,
these love letters you keep writing to your mother.

Our Neighbor Girl is Bathing Her Calf for the Fair

and the sky is blue satin above the tin roof's red.
Across the milking parlor's wall, this girl, her short

partner with wide eyes and funny shoes lean
into a late August day, while a dozen finches hum,

Oh how we danced on the night we were wed.

(Where's Diego Rivera when you need him?)
Whirls of palm circles make a drowsy calf, one

who doesn't mind a leather bridle, licks the princess,
uses a sandpaper tongue, likes her wand's cool water.

I watch the bath, all its twists and turns, random paths
of lathered swirls, her thumbs and fingers smooth his spotty

tuxedo. The puddle's soapy beard grows. Shannon's easy
smile and laughter before she lets go the garden hose

to hug and hug her black-faced calf, neck-to-neck.
Her arms, pink roses in a winner's garland.

A woman, her face pressed into the barn's wet bouquet.

This calf? I want it to be my life.

David and Jeanne Bryner

ABOUT THE AUTHOR

Jeanne Bryner's family was part of Appalachia's outmigration, and she considers living close to a dairy farm these many years a blessing. A graduate of Trumbull Memorial Hospital's School of Nursing and Kent State University's Honors College, she has received awards for community service, nursing and writing. She worked as a staff nurse in pediatrics, Med-Surg, ICU, ER, Immediate Care, Periop-Pool, the IV team and Vlad Pediatrics where babies and children arrived like field flowers.

Her prose and poetry appear in national and international journals, anthologies and textbooks, but working with her students, helping them find their voice has greatly enriched her life and writing. To facilitate the healing power of language, Jeanne teaches writing workshops in cancer support groups, nursing homes, schools and universities. Her books include *Breathless, Blind Horse: Poems, Eclipse: Stories, Tenderly Lift Me: Nurses Honored, Celebrated and Remembered, The Wedding of Miss Meredith Mouse, No Matter How Many Windows* (2011 Tillie Olsen Award from the Working Class Studies Association,) *Smoke: Poems* (2012 American Journal of Nursing Book of the Year award,) and *Early Farming Woman.*

Jeanne's poetry has been adapted for the stage and performed in Ohio, Kentucky, West Virginia, New York, Texas, Pennsylvania and Edinburgh, Scotland. Her new play, *Foxglove Canyon*, was first performed in Akron at Summa Healthcare's Humanities conference under the direction of Russell Zampino. With the support of Hiram College's Center for Literature, Medicine and Biomedical Humanities, her nursing poetry has been adapted and performed by Verb Ballets, Cleveland, Ohio. She has received writing fellowships from Bucknell University, the Ohio Arts Council (1997, 2007) and Vermont Studio Center.

Judy Waid

About the Artist

Judy Waid is retired after forty years of nursing. A graduate of Trumbull Memorial Hospital's School of Nursing, wife and mother, she has always pursued her love of art. She studied at Kent State University and the Cleveland Institute of Art, and has received several art awards.

The Ohio Nurses Association commissioned her to design medallions based on nursing personalities and historical moments in nursing now in museums, universities, private collections and in the textbook , *Nursing, The Finest Art*. Her portraits of prominent women in the Warren-Youngstown area are well-known and on display at the Warren Trumbull County Public Library and the Harriett Upton House. A member of the Trumbull Art Gallery and its portrait group, she lives with her husband in Howland, Ohio.

ACKNOWLEDGMENTS CONTINUED

Thanks to my fine neighbors, Bertha, Theo, Susan, Richard, Daniel, Jenny and Shannon Montgomery for allowing me to use their names in these poems related to their lives and work on a third-generation Ohio dairy farm. To the readers and listeners who commented on these poems, I thank the following mentors and friends: Maggie Anderson, Katherine Orr, Alice Cone, Diane Gilliam, Sue Johnson and Ron Houchin. To the women who first called me an artist, Elizabeth Hoobler, Vivian Pemberton and Gloria Young, eternal thanks. Continued gratitude to Robert Wick and Walter Wick for their friendship, support, and the Wick Poetry Program at Kent State University. For my fellowship at Bucknell University, I thank Mr. Jack Stadler. Many thanks to Vermont Studio Center for a 2006 residency and 2009 Fellowship which kept my pen in forward motion. I am grateful to the Ohio Arts Council for two Individual Excellence grants. Again, I thank my son, Gary Michael Bryner and daughter, Summar Leigh Bryner, for the hard brilliance of a Mother's journey. And to David, who reads every single draft, thanks and thanks for your love and support.

"August 1976: Bertha Welcomes Me to The Neighborhood" was chosen for a performance art piece from *Every River on Earth*, Friday, October 16, 2015, Kahl Theatre in the Vern Riffe Center for the Arts, Shawnee State University, Portsmouth, Ohio, director, Dr. John Houston, musical director, Dr. Barnhart.

"My Husband Was in a Hospital Bed" is for Ron Birchak, Stew Bryant, Sonny Bryner, Bob Holesko, Joe Pinkard and Arvie Staton.

In memory of Kevin Brody, Bertha Montgomery, Theo Montgomery, Donnie Morrow and Charles Gerald Stiles.

Recent Books by Bottom Dog Press

HARMONY SERIES

Both Shoes Off: Poems by Jeanne Bryner, 112 pgs, $16
Stolen Child: A Novel by Suzanne Kelly, 338 pgs. $18
The Canary : A Novel by Michael Loyd Gray, 196 pgs. $18
On the Flyleaf: Poems by Herbert Woodward Martin, 106 pgs. $16
The Harmonist at Nightfall: Poems of Indianab
by Shari Wagner, 114 pgs. $16
Painting Bridges: A Novel by Patricia Averbach, 234 pgs. $18
Ariadne & Other Poems by Ingrid Swanberg, 120 pgs. $16
The Search for the Reason Why: New and Selected Poems
by Tom Kryss, 192 pgs. $16
Kenneth Patchen: Rebel Poet in America
by Larry Smith, Revised 2nd Edition, 326 pgs. Cloth $28
Selected Correspondence of Kenneth Patchen,
Edited with introduction by Allen Frost, Paper $18/ Cloth $28
Awash with Roses: Collected Love Poems of Kenneth Patchen
Eds. Laura Smith and Larry Smith
With introduction by Larry Smith, 200 pgs. $16

HARMONY COLLECTIONS AND ANTHOLOGIES

d.a.levy and the mimeograph revolution
Eds. Ingrid Swanberg and Larry Smith, 276 pgs. $20
Come Together: Imagine Peace
Eds. Ann Smith, Larry Smith, Philip Metres, 204 pgs. $16
Evensong: Contemporary American Poets on Spirituality
Eds. Gerry LaFemina and Chad Prevost, 240 pgs. $16
America Zen: A Gathering of Poets
Eds. Ray McNiece and Larry Smith, 224 pgs. $16
Family Matters: Poems of Our Families
Eds. Ann Smith and Larry Smith, 232 pgs. $16

Breathing the West: Great Basin Poems
by Liane Ellison Norman, 80 pgs. $16
Maggot : A Novel by Robert Flanagan, 262 pgs. $18
American Poet: A Novel by Jeff Vande Zande, 200 pgs. $18
The Way-Back Room: Memoir of a Detroit Childhood
by Mary Minock, 216 pgs. $18
Strangers in America: A Novel by Erika Meyers, 140 pgs. $16
Riders on the Storm: A Novel by Susan Streeter Carpenter, 404 pgs. $18
Landscape with Fragmented Figures: A Novel
by Jeff Vande Zande, 232 pgs. $16
The Big Book of Daniel: Collected Poems
by Daniel Thompson, 340 pgs. Paper $18/ Cloth $22;

Recent Books By Bottom Dog Press

Appalachian Writing Series
Brown Bottle: A Novel by Sheldon Lee Compton, 162 pgs. $18
A Small Room with Trouble on My Mind
by Michael Henson, 164 pgs. $18
Drone String: Poems by Sherry Cook Stanforth, 92 pgs. $16
Voices from the Appalachian Coalfields by Mike Yarrow and Ruth
Yarrow, Photos by Douglas Yarrow, 152 pgs. $17
Wanted: Good Family by Joseph G. Anthony, 212 pgs. $18
Sky Under the Roof: Poems by Hilda Downer, 126 pgs. $16
Green-Silver and Silent: Poems by Marc Harshman, 90 pgs. $16
The Homegoing: A Novel by Michael Olin-Hitt, 180 pgs. $18
*She Who Is Like a Mare: Poems of Mary Breckinridge and
the Frontier Nursing Service* by Karen Kotrba, 96 pgs. $16
Smoke: Poems by Jeanne Bryner, 96 pgs. $16
Broken Collar: A Novel by Ron Mitchell, 234 pgs. $18
The Pattern Maker's Daughter: Poems
by Sandee Gertz Umbach, 90 pages $16
The Free Farm: A Novel by Larry Smith, 306 pgs. $18
Sinners of Sanction County: Stories by Charles Dodd White, 160 pgs. $17
Learning How: Stories, Yarns & Tales by Richard Hague, 216 pgs. $18
The Long River Home: A Novel
by Larry Smith, 230 pgs. cloth $22; paper $16
Eclipse: Stories by Jeanne Bryner, 150 pgs. $16

Appalachian Anthologies
Appalachia Now: Short Stories of Contemporary Appalachia
Eds. Charles Dodd White and Larry Smith, 160 pgs. $18
Degrees of Elevation: Short Stories of Contemporary Appalachia
Eds. Charles Dodd White and Page Seay, 186 pgs. $18

Bottom Dog Press, Inc.
P.O. Box 425 /Huron, Ohio 44839
http://smithdocs.net

CPSIA information can be obtained
at www.ICGtesting.com
Printed in the USA
FFOW02n1803060416
23034FF

9 781933 964843